One Hour for My Priest

One Hour for My Priest

A PRAYER COMPANION

Tina Jost

Our Sunday Visitor
Huntington, Indiana

Nihil Obstat
Msgr. Michael Heintz, Ph.D.
Censor Librorum

Imprimatur
✠ Kevin C. Rhoades
Bishop of Fort Wayne-South Bend
May 23, 2024

The *Nihil Obstat* and *Imprimatur* are official declarations that a book is free from doctrinal or moral error. It is not implied that those who have granted the *Nihil Obstat* and *Imprimatur* agree with the contents, opinions, or statements expressed.

Scripture texts in this work are taken from the *New American Bible*, revised edition © 2010, 1991, 1986, 1970 Confraternity of Christian Doctrine, Washington, D.C. and are used by permission of the copyright owner. All Rights Reserved. No part of the *New American Bible* may be reproduced in any form without permission in writing from the copyright owner.

Excerpts from the English translation of the *Catechism of the Catholic Church* for use in the United States of America Copyright © 1994, United States Catholic Conference, Inc.—Libreria Editrice Vaticana. Used with Permission. English translation of the *Catechism of the Catholic Church*: Modifications from the Editio Typica copyright © 1997, United States Conference of Catholic Bishops—Libreria Editrice Vaticana.

Every reasonable effort has been made to determine copyright holders of excerpted materials and to secure permissions as needed. If any copyrighted materials have been inadvertently used in this work without proper credit being given in one form or another, please notify Our Sunday Visitor in writing so that future printings of this work may be corrected accordingly.

Copyright © 2024 by Tina Jost
29 28 27 26 25 24   1 2 3 4 5 6 7 8 9

Our Sunday Visitor Publishing Division
Our Sunday Visitor, Inc.
200 Noll Plaza
Huntington, IN 46750
www.osv.com
1-800-348-2440

ISBN: 978-1-63966-214-2 (Inventory No. T2903)
1. RELIGION—Christian Living—Prayer.
2. RELIGION—Prayerbooks—Christian.
3. RELIGION—Christianity—Catholic.
LCCN: 2024942344

Cover design: Tyler Ottinger
Cover art: Adobe Stock
Interior design: Amanda Falk
Interior art: istock and Alamy

Printed in the United States of America

*To the Holy Trinity: May you be glorified
through this work, and may it lead others to you!*

The priesthood is the love of the heart of Jesus. When you see a priest, think of our Lord Jesus Christ.

— St. John Marie Vianney

Contents

Introduction

You've picked up this booklet to pray for a priest that you know. Our priests are such a gift from God, and you understand the importance of our prayers for them. Without our beloved priests, we wouldn't be able to receive Jesus in the Blessed Sacrament or to pray in adoration.

In this prayer companion, I use the words *mystery* and *moments* quite a bit. These terms and this prayer companion have been inspired by the Saint Andrew Novena, and in it, we pray:

Hail and blessed be the *hour* and *moment* in which the Son of God was born of the most pure Virgin Mary, at midnight, in Bethlehem, in the piercing cold. *In that hour* vouchsafe, I beseech thee, O my God, to hear my prayer and grant my desires, through the merits of Our Savior Jesus Christ, and of his Blessed Mother. Amen.

This prayer is what I refer to as a Divine Moment. Here we are pleading with God at the moment the Son of God was born. We are asking the Holy Trinity, now and at the moment of Jesus' birth, to help us in some way. This holy hour booklet will contain many of these Divine Moments. We will be pleading with God for the soul of our priest and continually bringing him, into different moments of Salvation History.

We can pray this way because our human under-standing of time is (necessarily) a created construct of limits. God exists completely outside of time, and thus outside of those limits. The *Catechism of the Catholic Church* describes God as being "beyond space and time" (205). So, Jesus' nativity is not just something that did happen but, in the deposit of eternity, is continuously happening. The crucifixion of Our Lord has happened and is happening. His resurrection has happened and is happening now. We acknowledge this every time we pray, "As it was in the beginning, is now, and ever shall be." We enter into this great mystery at each Mass. The mystery surpasses our understanding, yet we embrace it with faith and joy, and we will enter into it throughout this book.

This booklet is intended to be prayed during a holy hour in front of Jesus Christ in the Blessed Sacrament, whether in the tabernacle or during adoration. This prayer companion will lead you through an hour of prayer for the soul of one priest — your pastor, a priest in your diocese, or any priest you feel called to pray for.

There are two different holy hours to choose from in this booklet:

1. Begin with the section titled "In the Presence of God," then pray the "One-minute Meditations," and then continue with one set of the Mysteries of the Rosary. Finish with the prayers in the final section, "Help Him."
2. Begin with the section titled "In the Presence of God," then pray the Sorrowful Mysteries of the Rosary (beginning on page 53) and the Stations of the Cross.

Let the Holy Spirit guide you to have flexibility in your prayers. Complete the hour with the closing prayer at the end of the book.

Pray with me, and let's bring your priest, Father _____, with us into the mystery of God.

In the Presence of God

Amen. Blessing and glory, wisdom and thanksgiving,
honor, power, and might
be to our God forever and ever. Amen.

— Revelation 7:12

Before we begin, let's remember that we are in the awesome presence of God. We believe that he sees and hears us. It is such a blessing to have this time with him. If you cannot be physically in a church before the Blessed Sacrament, you can, as St. John Vianney says, "fly before the tabernacle" in your mind.

As you begin this time of prayer, remove all distractions you can control. For example, silence your phone, etc. If your mind wanders during your prayers, don't feel discouraged. Simply remind yourself that you are in the presence of an understanding God, ask your Guardian Angel to help focus your prayer, and pick up where you left off. God hears our prayers, no matter how imperfect they are.

When you are ready to commit this hour's intercession toward the good of the priest you want to pray for, begin.

Make the Sign of the Cross.

Pray: Jesus, I believe you are truly here in the Sacrament of Divine Love. Please accept my prayers as I offer this hour for Father _____. I bring Father _____ humbly before you, O God. Please make this time fruitful for your honor and his soul. Holy God, may your blessing be upon Father _____ now and for all eternity.

Father _____'s Guardian Angel, lead him to Jesus.
Blessed Mother, lead him to Jesus.
Holy Spirit, guide and lead him all the days of his life.
Saint Joseph, pray for him.
Saint Benedict, pray for him.
Saint _____, Father _____'s holy patron, pray for him.
All saints in heaven, pray for him.
Lord, you know all our weaknesses. Please heal Father _____ in every way he needs to be healed, in his

mind, body, and soul.

Bless his vocation.

Help him to do your will; help him to be as holy as you desire him to be.

You who exist outside of time, bless him, every year of his life.

Jesus Christ, Son of the living God, have mercy on him, a sinner.

Glory to you, God, at this moment in the tabernacle and for all eternity!

Placing all of Father _____'s intentions at the foot of the cross, we pray:

Glory Be …

Our Father …

Blessed Mother, Our Lady Star of the Sea, please take these intentions to Jesus.

Sub Tuum Praesidium

We fly to your patronage, O holy Mother of God. Despise not our petitions in our necessities, but deliver us always from all dangers, O glorious and blessed Virgin Mary. Amen.

Come, Holy Spirit!

Thank You, God!

Five One-Minute Meditations

I will praise you with all my heart,
glorify your name forever, Lord my God.

— Psalm 86:12

In this section, we will pray for our priest with five one-minute meditations. We will use what I call a "rosary timer." Using your rosary beads, think of each bead as one second in a minute. Beginning at the crucifix, move your fingers along each rosary bead at a steady beat. When you have moved your fingers around the whole rosary, it will equate to roughly a minute. Sometimes you may feel like your hands are moving faster than your words. In that case, just take a breath and slow yourself down. Savor the privilege of praying in the moment, and

17

with focus. Come up with your own specific intentions for these meditations, and they will be a prayer you can do anywhere at any time. I will be giving suggestions for each meditation, but it is best if you think of your particular priest and customize these prayers.

First Minute: "Thank you, God, for this priest"

Using your rosary, recite these words on each bead. It's that simple: Bring to mind the priest you are praying for and thank God for him. Say, "Thank you, God, for Father _____." Repeat this prayer on each bead of the rosary.

Second Minute: "Thank you, God, for ... [specifics]"

This meditation is about taking your thanksgiving further. Hold Father _____ in your mind. While in God's presence, give heartfelt thanks for the priest's specific qualities, things he has accomplished, or blessings that have come through the hands of this servant of God. Over time, this meditation could take on the rhythm and repetitive characteristics of a litany as you add new considerations or leave others out (as you are free to do), in hopes of best serving your priest.

After each specific thing you're thankful for, say,

"Thank you, God!"

For Father _____'s life ... **Thank you, God!**
For his parents ...
For his godparents or sponsors ...
For all the people who raised him ...
For the priests who influenced him ...
For all those who taught him ...
For those who have inspired him ...
For the ancestors who prayed for him ...
For the saints who intercede for him ...
For his intelligence ...
For his education ...
For his "yes" to his vocation ...
For his dedication to your service ...
For all the sacraments he has received ...
For all his personal strengths ...
For his healthy mind, body, and soul ...
For his eyes to see you ...
For his ears to hear you ...
For his hands to serve ...
For his mouth to proclaim your word ...
For his positive influence on others ...
For his teaching ...
For his example ...

For his laughter …
For his goodness …
For his gentleness …
For his generosity …
For his witness …
For the courage you give him …
For giving me the opportunity to pray for him …

Write your unique reasons to give thanks for your priest here. What are some blessings that have come from his priesthood?

Third Minute: "Thank you, God" appreciation

When we appreciate something, our thanksgiving goes deeper. When we thank God and show him our appreciation for someone, we tell him that we value or cherish this person. When Jesus healed the ten lepers, only one returned and thanked him (see Lk 17:11–19). The leper who returned knew the value of his healing. He understood what it was like to be an outcast, to be in pain, and to be suffering. When he was healed, he was profoundly grateful to have a life that could be fully lived again.

This is the kind of appreciation we want to have for the gift of Father _____. Pondering what a blessing this particular priest is, or, conversely, thinking of what it would be like without him, can help you value him more deeply.

Stop a moment and appreciate the *gift* of this priest. Think about the value he brings to the people and community he serves. Using the following suggestions, it will equal roughly one minute. (Note: You can also take the specifics used in the previous thanksgiving meditation and add appreciation. Since each priest we pray for differs, personalization matters.)

Respond to the following with, **"Thank you, God!"**

Thank You, God, for Father _____. We sincerely
appreciate the blessing of this priest. **Thank you,
God!**

We appreciate that he is a good, dedicated, faithful
priest …

We appreciate that the Holy Spirit works through him
as he acts *in persona Christi* …

We appreciate that he is a loyal servant …

We appreciate every Mass he offers …

We appreciate that he offers us the sacraments …

We appreciate all his unknown sacrifices …

We appreciate that he continually teaches us …

We appreciate that he is healthy …

We appreciate all his unique gifts …

We appreciate his intelligence …

We appreciate his kindness …

We appreciate his guidance …

We appreciate his homilies …

We appreciate his influence on our family …

We appreciate that he has been a loving father to us …

We appreciate his fatherly advice …

We appreciate his many hours of unseen work …

We appreciate that he said "yes" to his vocation …

We appreciate that he leads us closer to you …

We appreciate each moment that he serves as a priest …

We appreciate the unseen blessings that have come
    from his life …
We appreciate that he gives us the Eucharist …
We value and cherish the gift of this priest. We really
    appreciate it! …

Write some of the things you appreciate about the gift of
your priest here:

Fourth Minute: "Thank you, God, for future blessings"

Many saints have talked about giving thanks to God before something happens. Perhaps the most well-known is Bl. Solanus Casey, who was known to say, "Thank God ahead of time!" Jesus taught us the importance of praying confidently when he said, "Therefore I tell you, all that you ask for in prayer, believe that you will receive it and it shall be yours" (Mk 11:24). Thanking God for future blessings upon your priest shows our belief that God will continue to give him graces in way that is beyond our understanding.

In this meditation, we will consider future blessings for Father _____, thanking God beforehand. Your priest will receive many gifts from God through his vocation, and God will use his life to bless others. If it's God's will, what are some possible joyful life events he may have in the future? Gifts that will be given to him? Unseen graces?

You can pray this meditation in several ways. Using your "rosary timer" again, you can pray, "Thank you, God, for future blessings for Father _____." You could also say, "Thank you, God, for the blessings that will be given to Father _____," or "Thank you for the blessings that will be given to others through his priesthood and life."

You can use the suggestions below, but be sure to personalize this meditation so it suits your particular priest.

Respond to the following with, **"Thank you, God!"**

For all the people, Father _____ will lead to you …
Thank you, God!

For the future graces he will receive through the sacraments …

For the lessons he will teach in his homilies …

For the many blessings he will receive each day …

For the gifts that will be given to him …

For the good health of his body, mind, and soul …

For the advice he will give to others …

For all the babies he will baptize …

For all the Masses he will offer …

For all the confessions he will hear …

For all the marriages he will bless …

For all his visits to the sick …

For the joy others will bring him …

For the blessing of friendships in his life …

For all the insights you will give him …

For the legacy he will leave us …

For the continued hope for a life with you for all eternity …

Thank you, God, for these future blessings, graces, and gifts! (Write some future blessings for your priest here.)

Fifth Minute: Glory to you, God, at this moment

When we pray the Rosary, we meditate on the mysteries in the life of Jesus and Mary. In this minute, we'll meditate on these or other occasions within the Gospel, with attention to the soul of our priest.

It's such a mystery to us, but we believe God's time transcends our own in ways beyond our understanding. This is a holy mystery worth pondering. Working within this minute, we will adore and praise God and then ask him to remember our priest at one specific gospel moment. While there are countless ways to do this, here is the method I recommend to start.

In the Gloria we pray during the Holy Sacrifice of the Mass, we say, "Glory to God in the highest! … We praise you, we bless you, we adore you, we glorify you. We give you thanks for your great glory!" We will use this prayer to go more deeply into our intercessions, petitioning God, who is outside of time.

Below are examples of a few ways to pray this meditation using the Gloria. Please personalize this meditation for your priest.

1. Use the mysteries of the Rosary.

Contemplate a mystery of the Rosary, for example,

the Annunciation. Visualize the scene. Now praise and adore God. "The Angel of the Lord declared unto Mary, and she conceived of the Holy Spirit. Glory to you, God, at the moment of the Incarnation. We praise you, we bless you, we adore you, we glorify you! We give you thanks for your great glory! In that moment, have mercy on Father _____."

2. Use scenes from Scripture.

Call to mind a scene relevant to your priest or the liturgical season. For example, contemplate the moment when Jesus healed a leper. Read the Scripture passage: "And then a leper approached, did him homage, and said, 'Lord, if you wish, you can make me clean.' He stretched out his hand, touched him, and said, 'I will do it. Be made clean.' His leprosy was cleansed immediately" (Mt 8:2–3). Visualize the moment. Now praise and adore God. "Glory to you, God in this moment of healing. We praise you, we bless you, we adore you, we glorify you! We give you thanks for your great glory. Through this action, heal Father _____ and cleanse him from his sins."

3. Use the life of Christ

To keep the meditation to one minute, you can either

enter into this praise of his glory (see Eph 1:12) by using the suggestions above, or you can say the following litany based on the life of Christ.

Ponder and visualize one moment with God and the priest you are praying for. Bring him to God. Go slowly. Praise and thank God!

After the first two invocations, respond with, **"Bless, heal, and have mercy on him."**

Glory to you, God, for all eternity! Thank you, God! We praise you, God!

Glory to you, Jesus! At your Incarnation, bless, heal, and have mercy on Father _____.

Glory to you, Jesus! At the moment of your birth ... **Bless, heal, and have mercy on him.**

Glory to you, Jesus! In your childhood ...

Glory to you, Jesus! As you work beside Saint Joseph ...

Glory to you, Jesus! When you preach your Sermon on the Mount ...

Glory to you, Jesus! In your hours of agony ...

Glory to you, Jesus! As you suffer and die for us on the cross ...

Glory to you, Jesus! At your resurrection...

Glory to you, Jesus! As you greet your disciples, saying, "Peace be with you."

Glory to you, Jesus! At your ascension into heaven …
Glory to you, Jesus! Seated at the right hand of the Father
  …
Glory to you, Jesus! In all the tabernacles of the world …
Glory to you, Jesus! In the hands of every priest on the
  altar …
Glory to you, Jesus! In every Eucharist I have received …
Glory to you, Jesus! We praise you now and for all eter-
  nity!

What other moments in the life of Jesus would you like
to add?

_____

_____

_____

_____

_____

_____

_____

The Holy Rosary

Most blessed are you among women, and
blessed is the fruit of your womb.

— Luke 1:42

In this section and the following three, we will pray the Rosary for our particular priest. As you read the Scripture associated with each mystery, place yourself within the scene. Imagine the sounds, the sights, and the emotions you feel as though you are there. We will bring Father _____ into the crux of the scene and ask God to bless him at the very moment it took place. Take it slowly. Ask Jesus and Mary to help you sustain your focus, to best help your priest in his vocation. If you need them, the prayers of the Rosary can be found in the appendix at the end of this book. Come, Holy Spirit!

Opening Prayer

Blessed Mother, you loved your Son even more than we could possibly comprehend. Thank you for being a mother to us all. Please hear our prayers for this priest who has given his life to the service of God and his Church.

Holy God, as we pray with the Queen of Heaven, we know we are before you here in the Sacrament of Divine Love. Hear our pleas for Father _____ throughout this Rosary. On behalf of this priest, we beg you to give him all the graces necessary to live in close union with your Son. Help him to fulfill his vocation faithfully so that he might one day hear the words: "Well done, my good and faithful servant. Since you were faithful in small matters, I will give you great responsibilities. Come, share your master's joy" (Mt 25:23).

Now begin the prayers of the Rosary. There is an intention for your priest before each prayer of the Rosary.

Help Father _____ to have true reverence and awe in
    your sacred presence. **I believe in God, the Father**
    Almighty …
Help him to praise you now so he can rejoice with you
    for all eternity. **Our Father …**
Increase his faith. **Hail Mary …**

Increase his hope. **Hail Mary …**
Increase his love. **Hail Mary …**
Mother of God, intercede for him. **Glory Be …**

Joyful Mysteries

First Joyful Mystery: The Annunciation

In the sixth month, the angel Gabriel was sent from God to a town of Galilee called Nazareth, to a virgin betrothed to a man named Joseph, of the house of David, and the virgin's name was Mary. And coming to her, he said, "Hail, favored one! The Lord is with you." But she was greatly troubled at what was said and pondered what sort of greeting this might be. Then the angel said to her, "Do not be afraid, Mary, for you have found favor with God. Behold, you will conceive in your womb and bear a son, and you shall name him Jesus. He will be great and will be called Son of the Most High, and the Lord God will give him the throne of David his father, and he will rule over the house of Jacob forever, and of his kingdom there will be no end." (Luke 1:26–33)

Prayer

At the moment of the Incarnation, we cry out, "Hail, our king and Lord!" and exclaim from the depths of our hearts our love for you. In your kindness, remember this devoted priest in that very instant. Bless him now, as we honor you when you came to us as God-made-man.

Please help Father _____ to grow in holiness. **Our Father …**

Help him to find favor with you, our Triune God. **Hail Mary …**

Help him to discern your voice clearly. **Hail Mary …**

Help him to have obedience and humility in his vocation. **Hail Mary …**

Help him to say "yes" to little mortifications. **Hail Mary …**

Help him to be pure like Mary. **Hail Mary …**

Help him to turn to Mary when he is troubled. **Hail Mary …**

Help him to be not afraid. **Hail Mary …**

Help him to have gratitude for blessings. **Hail Mary …**

Help him to remember nothing is impossible with you. **Hail Mary …**

Help him to serve you faithfully. **Hail Mary …**

Help him to shepherd his flock. **Glory be …**

Help him to be prudent when making decisions. **O my Jesus …**

The Second Joyful Mystery: The Visitation

During those days Mary set out and traveled to the hill country in haste to a town of Judah, where she entered the house of Zechariah and greeted Elizabeth. When Elizabeth heard Mary's greeting, the infant leaped in her womb, and Elizabeth, filled with the holy Spirit, cried out in a loud voice and said, "Most blessed are you among women, and blessed is the fruit of your womb." (Luke 1:39–42)

Prayer

Jesus, at the instant when St. John the Baptist recognized you in the womb of our Blessed Mother, remember this priest! We praise you, Jesus, and exclaim, "My Lord and My God!" We cry out with joy and love for you, our infant king; remember Father _____ at the very moment of this blessed Visitation!

Please help Father _____ to bring Jesus to others. **Our Father …**

Help him to serve others promptly. **Hail Mary …**

Help him to bring consolation to those in need. **Hail Mary ...**

Give him loyal friends. **Hail Mary ...**

Help him to venerate your Holy Name. **Hail Mary ...**

Help him to be a living witness of great devotion to you. **Hail Mary ...**

Give him clarity when he is uncertain. **Hail Mary ...**

Help him to be joyful and generous. **Hail Mary ...**

Help him to persevere in his faith. **Hail Mary ...**

Help him to give thanks at all times, in goodness and adversity. **Hail Mary ...**

Help him to be conscious that he is always before the face of God. **Hail Mary ...**

Help him to live his vocation to the best of his ability. **Glory be ...**

Help him to practice holy justice. **O my Jesus ...**

The Third Joyful Mystery: The Birth of Our Lord

In those days a decree went out from Caesar Augustus that the whole world should be enrolled. This was the first enrollment, when Quirinius was governor of Syria. So all went to be enrolled, each to his own town. And Joseph too went up from Galilee from the town of Nazareth to Judea, to the city of David that is called Bethlehem, because he was of the house and family of David, to be enrolled with Mary, his betrothed, who was with child. While they were there, the time came for her to have her child, and she gave birth to her firstborn son. She wrapped him in swaddling clothes and laid him in a manger, because there was no room for them in the inn. (Luke 2:1–7)

Prayer

The angels sang gloriously as they proclaimed your birth! In that exact moment, we beg you to remember your faithful servant. Help him to sing your praises and give glory to you! We shout, "Glory to God in the highest" at your coming, and we sing of your loving might with all the angels and saints for this priest. In this moment, remember him, and help him in his vocation.

Help Father _____ to adore you from the depths of his heart. **Our Father …**

Help him to proclaim the news of great joy. **Hail Mary …**
Help him to sing your praises. **Hail Mary …**
Help him to give you his every talent. **Hail Mary …**
Help him to seek your face forevermore. **Hail Mary …**
Help him to turn to Saint Joseph. **Hail Mary …**

Help his unbelief. **Hail Mary …**

Help him to exhibit heroic virtue. **Hail Mary …**

Help him to be genuinely considerate of others. **Hail Mary …**

Give him wisdom. **Hail Mary …**

Help him to grow in righteousness. **Hail Mary …**

Like the Wise Men, help him to honor you as king. **Glory be …**

Help him to grow in temperance. **O my Jesus …**

The Fourth Joyful Mystery: The Presentation in the Temple

> *When eight days were completed for his circumcision, he was named Jesus, the name given him by the angel before he was conceived in the womb. When the days were completed for their purification according to the law of Moses, they took him up to Jerusalem to present him to the Lord, just as it is written in the law of the Lord, "Every male that opens the womb shall be consecrated to the Lord," and to offer the sacrifice of "a pair of turtledoves or two young pigeons," in accordance with the dictate in the law of the Lord. (Luke 2:21–24)*

Prayer

We adore you, Jesus Christ, rejoicing in the hour of your presentation in the temple. We implore you from the depths of our souls to bless this priest. In this moment, we, like Anna and Simeon, recognize, honor, and esteem you as Our Lord and God. We exclaim, "You are the one true God!" Remember your priest in this instant of recognition and give him all the graces he needs now to do your holy will.

Help Father _____ when a sword pierces his heart. **Our Father …**

Help him to be obedient to his superiors. **Hail Mary …**

Help him to discern prudently when faced with a difficult decision. **Hail Mary …**

Help him during the difficult moments that only you see. **Hail Mary …**

Help him to do the little things that have a lasting impact on his soul. **Hail Mary …**

Help him to be dedicated to your service. **Hail Mary …**

Help him to administer the sacraments with reverence. **Hail Mary …**

Help him to be truly consecrated to the Sacred Heart of Jesus. **Hail Mary …**

Help him to be a light to others. **Hail Mary …**

Help him to listen to your voice. **Hail Mary …**
Help him to be hopeful and patient, like Anna. **Hail Mary …**
Help him to be righteous and devout, like Simeon. **Glory be …**
Help him to grow in fortitude. **O my Jesus …**

The Fifth Joyful Mystery:
The Finding of Jesus in the Temple

Each year his parents went to Jerusalem for the feast of Passover, and when he was twelve years old, they went up according to festival custom. After they had completed its days, as they were returning, the boy Jesus remained behind in Jerusalem, but his parents did not know it. Thinking that he was in the caravan, they journeyed for a day and looked for him among their relatives and acquaintances, but not finding him, they returned to Jerusalem to look for him. After three days they found him in the temple, sitting in the midst of the teachers, listening to them and asking them questions, and all who heard him were astounded at his understanding and his answers. (Luke 2:41–47)

Prayer

Joining your loving parents as they discovered you in the temple, we wonder at your ways, praising and adoring you, O God. Remember this priest in that moment of Mary and Joseph's relief and help him to find you anew each day. We thank you for your presence as we meditate on your reunion with Mary and Joseph. We beg you never to forget this dedicated servant. We shout in praise, "Glory to you, king of heavenly glory!"

Help Father _____ to follow the Church's authentic teachings and eternal truths. **Our Father ...**

Heighten his understanding. **Hail Mary ...**

Free him from all anxiety. **Hail Mary ...**

Help him to discern the promptings of the Holy Spirit. **Hail Mary ...**

Help him to love you throughout his life. **Hail Mary ...**

Help him to protect his flock. **Hail Mary ...**

Help him never to feel unduly lonely. **Hail Mary ...**

Strengthen him when he is tempted. **Hail Mary ...**

Help him to be humble. **Hail Mary ...**

Help him always to seek and find you. **Hail Mary ...**

Increase his love and commitment to you and to his vocation daily. **Hail Mary ...**

Inspire him to offer his sufferings for his people. **Glory**

be …

Instruct him to grow in the cardinal virtues. **O my Jesus …**

Guide him to eternity in heaven. **Hail, Holy Queen …**

In the name of the Father, and of the Son, and of the Holy Spirit. Amen.

The Luminous Mysteries

The First Luminous Mystery:
The Baptism in the Jordan

> *After Jesus was baptized, he came up from the water and behold, the heavens were opened [for him], and he saw the Spirit of God descending like a dove [and] coming upon him. And a voice came from the heavens, saying, "This is my beloved Son, with whom I am well pleased." (Matthew 3:16–17)*

Prayer

Jesus, as your divinity is revealed during your baptism, we venerate you as our God and king. Thank you for leading us! We praise you now and ask you to illuminate the mind and heart of this loyal priest. Wash away his sins, cleanse him, and renew his soul.

Help Father _____ to see the Holy Spirit at work in the Church. **Our Father …**

Give him sanctifying grace. **Hail Mary …**

Keep the light of faith alive in him. **Hail Mary …**

Help him to remember that he was created in your image. **Hail Mary …**

Guide him to look for your handiwork around him. **Hail Mary …**

Help him to seek Truth, Goodness, and Beauty. **Hail Mary …**

Help him to live in communion with you. **Hail Mary …**

Help him to bring the light of the living God to others. **Hail Mary …**

Remind him that he is sealed with the mark of Christ. **Hail Mary …**

Empower him to lead others to seek eternity with you. **Hail Mary …**

Help him to live with enthusiasm and joy. **Hail Mary …**

Help him to welcome the newly baptized members of the Church. **Glory be …**

Help him to administer the Sacrament of Baptism with love. **O my Jesus …**

The Second Luminous Mystery:
The Wedding Feast at Cana

On the third day there was a wedding in Cana in Galilee, and the mother of Jesus was there. Jesus and his disciples were also invited to the wedding. When the wine ran short, the mother of Jesus said to him, "They have no wine." [And] Jesus said to her, "Woman, how does your concern affect me? My hour has not yet come." His mother said to the servers, "Do whatever he tells you." (John 2:1–5)

Prayer

As you change water into wine, Lord Jesus Christ, we honor you as our Redeemer. We are amazed at this miraculous gift to everyone at the feast, and we celebrate with joy. Remember our good shepherd at this moment and help him to be transformed into the servant that you desire him to be. Help him to relish this mystery as he celebrates your sacraments, and to see your miracles when he least expects them.

Help Father _____ to trust in you when things seem bleak. **Our Father …**

Help him to be astounded by each of your miracles. **Hail Mary …**

Help him to look for little signs of you. **Hail Mary …**

Help him to wait patiently for the appointed hour. **Hail Mary …**

Help him to trust in your divinity. **Hail Mary …**

Help him to be elated by each glimpse of a new miracle. **Hail Mary …**

Help him to desire to know you, Jesus, more and more. **Hail Mary …**

Help him to remember to live in serenity with you. **Hail Mary …**

Mary, intercede for him. **Hail Mary …**

Help him to do whatever Jesus tells him (cf. Jn 2:5). **Hail Mary …**

Help him to follow Mary's trusting example. **Hail Mary …**

Give him the grace to believe in the Christ's Divine Revelation. **Glory be …**

Help him to prepare himself and his flock for heaven. **O my Jesus …**

The Third Luminous Mystery: The Proclamation of the Kingdom of God

> *After John had been arrested, Jesus came to Galilee proclaiming the gospel of God: "This is the time of fulfillment. The kingdom of God is at hand. Repent, and believe in the gospel." (Mark 1:14–15)*

Prayer

Jesus, as you undertake your ministry and begin to heal, teach, and lead us, we revere you. You announce that you are Messiah, and we praise and glorify you. Thank you for coming to redeem us, bringing all things to yourself. In this glorious moment, we adore you and ask you to heal, teach, and lead your priest into deeper union with you.

Help Father _____ to see that time with you is never wasted. **Our Father...**

Open his eyes so he can see you more clearly. **Hail Mary ...**

Help him to accept the Gospel with conviction. **Hail Mary ...**

Help him to build up your heavenly kingdom on earth. **Hail Mary ...**

Help him to teach with heavenly wisdom. **Hail Mary …**
Grant that his sermons will stir the hearts of his peo-
ple. **Hail Mary …**
Through your sacraments, give him a share in your
healing. **Hail Mary…**
Give him the graces necessary to use his time wisely.
Hail Mary …
Help him to encourage vocations to serve the Church.
Hail Mary …
May he tenderly lead his flock. **Hail Mary …**
Help him to repent and believe. **Hail Mary …**
Help him to turn back quickly if he goes astray. **Glory
be …**
Allow his words to soften hardened hearts. **O my
Jesus …**

*The Fourth Luminous Mystery:
The Transfiguration*

> *After six days Jesus took Peter, James, and John
> his brother, and led them up a high mountain by
> themselves. And he was transfigured before them;
> his face shone like the sun and his clothes became
> white as light. (Matthew 17:1–2)*

Prayer

Jesus, as your heavenly magnificence is revealed to the apostles, transform this priest into the man you call him to be. We praise you at this moment. We are astounded and silenced as we wonder at your divinity. In your resplendent transfiguration on this mountain, remember your priest, called to be a light for others. Help him to see your majesty and live with you in eternity!

Keep Father _____'s eyes open to your divine light.
Our Father ...
Let him see your glory. **Hail Mary ...**
Awaken him from all spiritual slumber. **Hail Mary ...**
Through him, may your light shine before men. **Hail Mary ...**
Help him to seek you if he becomes lukewarm. **Hail Mary ...**
Give him the desire, time, and resources to retreat and be with you. **Hail Mary ...**
Help him to listen to you attentively. **Hail Mary ...**
Help him to seek the light of your face. **Hail Mary ...**
As you commanded the apostles at the Transfiguration, help him to listen. **Hail Mary ...**
Help him not to be frightened amid the darkness. **Hail Mary ...**

Transform his life with the power of the Holy Spirit.
Hail Mary ...
Help him to stay awake and be ready. **Glory be ...**
Help him to allow you to lead. **O my Jesus ...**

The Fifth Luminous Mystery:
The Institution of the Eucharist

> *While they were eating, Jesus took bread, said the blessing, broke it, and giving it to his disciples said, "Take and eat; this is my body." (Matthew 26:26)*

Prayer

As you give us your sacred Body, Blood, Soul, and Divinity, we acclaim your greatness! In this moment, O my God, help your priest to earnestly serve you each time he offers the Holy Sacrifice. Give him all the graces necessary in his vocation and help him cherish the Eucharist, our greatest treasure on earth.

Help Father _____ to desire your Body and Blood eagerly. **Our Father ...**
Help him to long to spend time in your sacred presence. **Hail Mary ...**

Give him supernatural graces as he administers the Blessed Sacrament to us. **Hail Mary …**

Help his reverence to inspire and lead others to you. **Hail Mary …**

May he daily realize your magnificence. **Hail Mary …**

May he see your awesome wonder. **Hail Mary …**

Help his soul to burst with your praise! **Hail Mary …**

Give him solace and comfort in your presence. **Hail Mary …**

Help him to prepare worthily for the Eucharistic celebration. **Hail Mary …**

Fill his soul with abundant joy. **Hail Mary …**

Help him to cherish this covenant ratified in your Blood. **Hail Mary …**

Help him to await eagerly the kingdom that you have prepared for him. **Glory be …**

Help him to enlighten his flock to believe in this great mystery. **O my Jesus …**

Guide him to eternity in heaven. **Hail, Holy Queen …**

In the name of the Father, and of the Son, and of the Holy Spirit. Amen.

The Sorrowful Mysteries

The First Sorrowful Mystery:
The Agony in the Garden

> *Then he said to them, "My soul is sorrowful even to death. Remain here and keep watch with me." He advanced a little and fell prostrate in prayer, saying, "My Father, if it is possible, let this cup pass from me; yet, not as I will, but as you will." When he returned to his disciples he found them asleep. He said to Peter, "So you could not keep watch with me for one hour?" (Matthew 26:38–40)*

Prayer

As you pray and suffer for us, our God and king, we praise you. We thank you for the drops of blood you shed for us in your agony. In your moment of unimaginable suffering, remember your steadfast servant; help him when he feels tempted or weak.

Give Father _____ grace when he is sorrowful. **Our Father …**

Inspire him to keep watch with you. **Hail Mary …**

Help him to trust in the Father's will. **Hail Mary ...**
Help him to be faithful to his daily prayers. **Hail Mary ...**
Give him the words to comfort those in distress. **Hail Mary ...**
Remind him to offer his suffering for others. **Hail Mary ...**
Help him to drink the cup he is given courageously. **Hail Mary ...**
When he is challenged, help him to find his strength in you. **Hail Mary ...**
Send him a holy angel when he is weak. **Hail Mary ...**
Give him fervent prayers. **Hail Mary ...**
Help him to be a powerful intercessor for his flock. **Hail Mary ...**
Help him not to enter into temptation. **Glory be ...**
Help him to persevere in prayer. **O my Jesus ...**

The Second Sorrowful Mystery:
The Scourging at the Pillar

> *They shouted again, "Crucify him." Pilate said to them, "Why? What evil has he done?" They only shouted the louder, "Crucify him." So Pilate, wishing to satisfy the crowd, released Barabbas to them and, after he had Jesus scourged, handed him over to be crucified. (Mark 15:13–15)*

Prayer

You are scourged, stripped, whipped, and tortured, Jesus, Our Lord and Savior. We watch with horrified sorrow and yet praise you in your glory. In your excruciating moment of pain and sadness, please remember this truehearted priest and help him in his suffering.

May you find no fault in Father _____ at the last Judgment. **Our Father …**

Fill him with hope when he feels betrayed. **Hail Mary …**

Help him to remain firm in his convictions. **Hail Mary …**

When he receives a blow, give him strength. **Hail Mary …**

Give him the grace to submit to your will, no matter the cost. **Hail Mary …**

If he is falsely accused, give him peace. **Hail Mary …**

Keep your divine life alive in his soul. **Hail Mary …**

When he is insulted, help him to remember what you endured, Jesus. **Hail Mary …**

Help him to embrace the challenges and difficulties that come with his vocation. **Hail Mary …**

When others are preferred, help him to offer thanks. **Hail Mary …**

Help him to remain silent when appropriate. **Hail Mary …**

When his wounds are deep, heal them. **Glory be …**

Protect him from sins of the flesh. **O my Jesus ...**

The Third Sorrowful Mystery: The Crowning with Thorns

> *Then the soldiers of the governor took Jesus inside the praetorium and gathered the whole cohort around him. They stripped off his clothes and threw a scarlet military cloak about him. Weaving a crown out of thorns, they placed it on his head, and a reed in his right hand. And kneeling before him, they mocked him, saying, "Hail, King of the Jews!" They spat upon him and took the reed and kept striking him on the head. And when they had mocked him, they stripped him of the cloak, dressed him in his own clothes, and led him off to crucify him. (Matthew 27:27–31)*

Prayer

You are our Redeemer, and we extol and honor you! You are crowned with thorns, and we worship you as the one true king. Especially within this moment of mockery and derision, we increase our praise, crying out, "Hail, King Jesus!" Please remember your servant, Father _____, and in this moment accompany him when he is pierced by sin.

Give Father _____ the graces necessary to pray for his persecutors. **Our Father ...**

If he loses everything, console him. **Hail Mary ...**

Help him to feel your presence when he is lonely. **Hail Mary ...**

Ease his pain. **Hail Mary ...**

Strengthen him when he is mocked or impugned. **Hail Mary ...**

Help him to "offer no resistance to one who is evil" (Mt 5:39). **Hail Mary ...**

Help him to turn the other cheek. **Hail Mary ...**

Help him to go two miles when obliged to go one. **Hail Mary ...**

Give him the grace to love his enemies. **Hail Mary ...**

Help him to pray for those who defile sacred things. **Hail Mary ...**

Crown him with compassion. **Hail Mary ...**

Help him to remember that his body is a temple of the Holy Spirit. **Glory be ...**

Remind him that all goodness comes from you. **O my Jesus ...**

The Fourth Sorrowful Mystery: The Carrying of the Cross

> *They pressed into service a passer-by, Simon, a Cyrenian, who was coming in from the country, the father of Alexander and Rufus, to carry his cross. They brought him to the place of Golgotha (which is translated Place of the Skull). (Mark 15:21–22)*

Prayer

As Simon picks up your cross, easing your burden, Lord, we praise you! We believe that you are the God-Man, here to save us. We want to comfort you. It pains us to watch you carry this cross, and we want to help, too. We thank you for your suffering and ask you even now, in this moment, to help your cherished priest bear his wearisome duties with zeal for your Church.

Help Father _____ not to bear hatred in his heart. **Our Father ...**

Help him to be slow to anger. **Hail Mary ...**

Keep him from holding on to grudges. **Hail Mary ...**

Lighten his load. **Hail Mary ...**

Help him to carry his daily cross. **Hail Mary ...**

Hasten to help him when it is too heavy for him. **Hail Mary …**

Lead him. **Hail Mary …**

Send him holy assistance when he is in need. **Hail Mary …**

Give him the supernatural strength to ease someone else's cross. **Hail Mary …**

Rescue him from the slavery of sin. **Hail Mary …**

Give him refreshment when the burden of life weighs heavy. **Hail Mary …**

When he is despised, give him your grace. **Glory be …**

Help him to receive the reward of everlasting life. **O my Jesus …**

The Fifth Sorrowful Mystery: The Crucifixion

It was now about noon and darkness came over the whole land until three in the afternoon because of an eclipse of the sun. Then the veil of the temple was torn down the middle. Jesus cried out in a loud voice, "Father, into your hands I commend my spirit"; and when he had said this he breathed his last. The centurion who witnessed what had happened glorified God and said, "This man was innocent beyond doubt." When all the people who had gathered for this spectacle saw what had hap-

*pened, they returned home beating their breasts;
but all his acquaintances stood at a distance, including the women who had followed him from
Galilee and saw these events. (Luke 23:44–49)*

Prayer

At the moment of your crucifixion, our Lord and
God, we praise you! We are terrified and saddened,
both for your sake and for our own, at the thought
of life without you. Yet we honor you in this moment as our king and God. We believe in you and
beg you, with tears in our eyes, to have mercy on this
priest who works *in persona Christi*. Remember him
and ask God our Father to forgive him for his sins.

Help Father _____ to be willing to die to self daily.
Our Father …
Give him unceasing gratitude to you. **Hail Mary …**
Help him to imitate you, our crucified Savior. **Hail
Mary …**
Give him a love like yours for his neighbors. **Hail Mary …**
Help him to trust in you when the pain is raw. **Hail
Mary …**
Give him hope in the darkness. **Hail Mary …**
When he is shaken, give him peace. **Hail Mary …**

Help him to forgive others. **Hail Mary …**

Help him to strive to do his best. **Hail Mary …**

Give him a passion for the truth. **Hail Mary …**

Help him to be diligent in caring for his flock. **Hail Mary …**

Increase his devotion and decrease pride in his heart. **Glory be …**

Help him to be a beacon of light, guiding others to you. **O my Jesus …**

Guide him to eternity in heaven. **Hail, Holy Queen …**

In the name of the Father, and of the Son, and of the Holy Spirit. Amen.

The Glorious Mysteries

The First Glorious Mystery: The Resurrection

> *But at daybreak on the first day of the week they took the spices they had prepared and went to the tomb. They found the stone rolled away from the tomb; but when they entered, they did not find the body of the Lord Jesus. While they were puzzling over this, behold, two men in dazzling garments appeared to them. They were terrified and bowed their faces to the ground. They said to*

them, "Why do you seek the living one among the dead?" (Luke 24:1–5)

Prayer

Jesus, you have risen as you foretold, alleluia! You have conquered death! At the moment of your resurrection, O Lord Jesus Christ, we shout joyfully; at this glorious event, we worship you. Remember your loyal minister now — in this instance of your great victory — and give him your everlasting peace.

Help Father _____ to keep his eyes on eternity. **Our Father ...**

Give him confidence. **Hail Mary ...**

Help him to instruct your people in the truth. **Hail Mary ...**

Deliver him from evil and sin. **Hail Mary ...**

Help him to spread the good news. **Hail Mary ...**

Help him to recognize you, Jesus, in others. **Hail Mary ...**

Give him faith in your healing power. **Hail Mary ...**

Give him the joy of the Resurrection. **Hail Mary ...**

Help him to encourage others when their faith is shaken. **Hail Mary ...**

Calm his fears. **Hail Mary ...**

Give him contagious joy! **Hail Mary ...**

Make him a radiant light for others. **Glory be ...**
Increase his patience. **O my Jesus...**

The Second Glorious Mystery: The Ascension of Our Lord

> *So then the Lord Jesus, after he spoke to them, was taken up into heaven and took his seat at the right hand of God. (Mark 16:19)*

Prayer

In the moment you ascended into heaven, Jesus, our Lord and God, we feel hope that we will see you again. We sing, "Glory to God in the highest, to you, our heavenly king!" During your ascension, have mercy on this priest and give him the necessary graces to follow you.

Help Father _____ when he feels the weight of his sin.
   Our Father ...
Give him your peace. **Hail Mary ...**
Help him when he is faced with a stressful situation. **Hail Mary ...**
Strengthen his faith in times of persecution. **Hail Mary ...**
Help him to believe the words you spoke. **Hail Mary ...**
Open his mind to the scriptures. **Hail Mary ...**

Give him your Sacred Heart. **Hail Mary …**
Strengthen his devotion to the Eucharist. **Hail Mary …**
Help him to remain in the state of grace. **Hail Mary …**
Help him to bring your peace wherever he goes. **Hail Mary …**
Help him to minister to the dying. **Hail Mary …**
Guide him on the right path for your name's sake. **Glory be …**
Help him to be kind. **O my Jesus …**

The Third Glorious Mystery: The Descent of the Holy Spirit

> *When the time for Pentecost was fulfilled, they were all in one place together. And suddenly there came from the sky a noise like a strong driving wind, and it filled the entire house in which they were. Then there appeared to them tongues as of fire, which parted and came to rest on each one of them. And they were all filled with the holy Spirit and began to speak in different tongues, as the Spirit enabled them to proclaim. (Acts of the Apostles 2:1–4)*

Prayer

You sent the Holy Spirit to the apostles, and they are astounded by your glorious wonders. We are so thankful for this permeating gift of the Holy Spirit! We praise you and give glory to you. In this moment, fill your servant with your Holy Spirit in your great kindness.

Holy Spirit, strengthen Father _____ and give him courage. **Our Father ...**

Fill his heart with your love. **Hail Mary ...**

Holy Spirit, enlighten him. **Hail Mary ...**

Help him to count his blessings in difficulties. **Hail Mary ...**

When he labors and is burdened, give him rest. **Hail Mary ...**

Holy Spirit, guide his words. **Hail Mary ...**

Holy Spirit, increase your gifts in him. **Hail Mary ...**

Help him to revere you, O Third Person of the Trinity. **Hail Mary ...**

Holy Spirit help him to trust in you. **Hail Mary ...**

Holy Spirit, help him to proclaim the Faith so that others might understand. **Hail Mary ...**

Holy Spirit, help him to convey divine truths effectively. **Hail Mary ...**

Come, Holy Spirit, fill the heart of this loyal priest. **Glory be ...**

Help him to grow in self-control. **O my Jesus ...**

The Fourth Glorious Mystery:
The Assumption of Mary

> *For he has looked upon his handmaid's lowliness;*
> *behold, from now on will all ages call me blessed.*
> *The Mighty One has done great things for me,*
> *and holy is his name. (Luke 1:48–49)*

Prayer

Glory to you, Holy and Undivided Trinity! As the Blessed Mother's body is assumed into heaven, we thank you. Now, we ask you to remember this shepherd, your priest, who follows the way of Mary. We thank you for granting us a share in her tender and motherly love and implore you to teach this priest how to follow her lead.

Help Father _____ to follow the way of Mary. **Our Father ...**

Help him to look to Mary, our model of strength. **Hail Mary ...**

Help him to be devoted to Mary. **Hail Mary ...**

Help him to turn to her every day. **Hail Mary ...**

Mary, be a mother to him. **Hail Mary ...**

Mary, take him into your immaculate heart. **Hail Mary …**
Mary, help him now and at the hour of his death. **Hail
Mary …**
Mary, be his refuge in times of trouble. **Hail Mary …**
Mary, lead him to Jesus. **Hail Mary …**
Help him to meditate on heavenly things. **Hail Mary …**
Help him to have self-discipline. **Hail Mary …**
Jesus, help him to forgive as you taught us. **Glory be …**
Help him to grow in holiness. **O my Jesus …**

The Fifth Glorious Mystery:
The Crowning of Our Lady, Queen of Heaven

> *A great sign appeared in the sky, a woman clothed
> with the sun, with the moon under her feet, and
> on her head a crown of twelve stars. (Revelation
> 12:1)*

Prayer
We praise you, God, in heaven and on earth! You honor
our Blessed Mother in heaven, crowning her as Queen
of Heaven. At this luminous moment of her coronation,
we thank you. We are so grateful to you for giving us
this shining star to guide us. We beg of you to help this
priest imitate Mary's fiat and follow her lead, praising

the Lamb of God for all eternity.

Give Father _____ all the graces he needs in his vocation. **Our Father …**

Help him to be a man of integrity. **Hail Mary …**

Increase his love of his vocation. **Hail Mary …**

Give him holy vigor. **Hail Mary …**

Mary, be his Queen. **Hail Mary …**

Mary, help him to pray. **Hail Mary …**

Give him supernatural knowledge. **Hail Mary …**

Help him to administer the sacrament of Reconciliation wisely. **Hail Mary …**

Help him to produce good fruit through his words and example. **Hail Mary …**

Help him to be a prudent teacher. **Hail Mary …**

Have mercy on him. **Hail Mary …**

Refresh his soul. **Glory Be …**

Help him to counsel others with selflessness and wisdom. **O my Jesus …**

Guide him to eternity in heaven. **Hail, Holy Queen …**

In the name of the Father, and of the Son, and of the Holy Spirit. Amen.

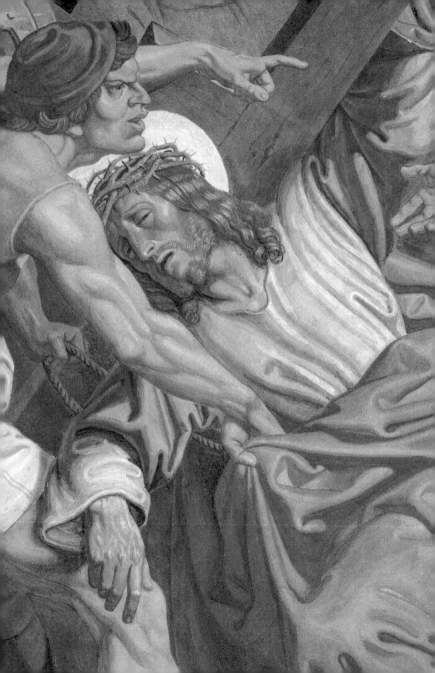

Stations of the Cross

When you lift up the Son of Man, then you will realize that I AM, and that I do nothing on my own, but I say only what the Father taught me.

— John 8:28

The Stations of the Cross can be prayed with or without walking the fourteen Stations in the church. If you are praying this holy hour in adoration with the Blessed Sacrament exposed, please pray the Stations while remaining in your pew.

Opening Prayer

As we enter this time of prayer and meditate on your suffering, death, and Resurrection, O Lord, Jesus Christ, please bless, heal, and have mercy on Father _____. In your suffering and in your glory, Lord, we believe in you!

Blessing, honor, and glory to you, Redeemer King!
Our Father …
Hail Mary …
Glory Be …

The First Station:
Jesus Is Condemned to Death

V: We adore you, O Christ, and we bless you.
R: Because by your Holy Cross, you have redeemed the world.

When the chief priests and the guards saw him they cried out, "Crucify him, crucify him!" Pilate said to them, "Take him yourselves and crucify him. I find no guilt in him." (John 19:6)

As the crowd shouts at you and yells, "Crucify him!" we offer you our praises. We exalt you and say, "Holy, Holy, Holy Lord God of hosts. . . . Blessed is he who comes in the name of the Lord. Hosanna in the highest." In the moment your torturers mock and hit you, look upon this priest who has given his life to serve you.

In this moment, Our Loving Lord Jesus Christ, we ask you to bless, heal, and have mercy on Father _____. Blessing, honor, and glory to you, Redeemer King!

Our Father …
Hail Mary …
Glory Be …

The Second Station: Jesus Takes His Cross

V: We adore you, O Christ, and we bless you.
R: Because by your Holy Cross, you have redeemed the world.

So they took Jesus, and carrying the cross himself, he went out to what is called the Place of the Skull, in Hebrew, Golgotha. (John 19:16–17)

You are carrying your cross, and we watch in silence, honoring you as our king. Now, instead of riding a donkey and hearing shouts of praise, you hear the calls of those who want you to suffer and die. As you begin your walk to Calvary, please look kindly upon this priest, who carries many burdens known to you alone.

In this moment, Our Loving Lord Jesus Christ, we ask you to bless, heal, and have mercy on Father _____.
Blessing, honor, and glory to you, Redeemer King!

Our Father …
Hail Mary …

Glory Be …

The Third Station: Jesus Falls the First Time

V: We adore you, O Christ, and we bless you.

R: Because by your Holy Cross, you have redeemed the world.

Though the just fall seven times, they rise again. (Proverbs 24:16)

The weight of the cross is too heavy to bear, and you fall to the ground. At the moment of your first fall, we want to give glory to you, our heavenly king. This priest, who has given his life to serve you, falls often and needs your help. In your kindness, give him the necessary graces to pick himself up, persevere, and keep going.

In this moment, Our Loving Lord Jesus Christ, we ask you to bless, heal, and have mercy on Father _____. Blessing, honor, and glory to you, Redeemer King!

Our Father …
Hail Mary …
Glory Be …

The Fourth Station: Jesus Meets His Mother

V: We adore you, O Christ, and we bless you.

R: Because by your Holy Cross, you have redeemed the world.

When Jesus saw his mother and the disciple there whom he loved, he said to his mother, "Woman, behold, your son." Then he said to the disciple, "Behold, your mother." And from that hour the disciple took her into his home. (John 19:26–27)

Your mother is near the torturous path to your crucifixion, Jesus. Though she never says a word, we know that her heart is pierced as she watches you suffer. Thank you for giving us such a steadfast mother! This priest, one of your favored sons, needs your mother, too. Help him to call on her when he is struggling in any way.

In this moment, Our Loving Lord Jesus Christ, we ask you to bless, heal, and have mercy on Father _____. Blessing, honor, and glory to you, Redeemer King!

Our Father …
Hail Mary …
Glory Be …

The Fifth Station: Jesus Is Helped by Simon

V: We adore you, O Christ, and we bless you.
R: Because by your Holy Cross, you have redeemed the

world.

As they were going out, they met a Cyrenian named Simon; this man they pressed into service to carry his cross (Matthew 27:32).

Jesus, we are so grateful that you are given a small break from your struggle when Simon assists with your cross. The agony is relieved a little as the weight shifts onto another. In your kindness, Lord, send your priest holy help when the task he is given requires aid from others.

In this moment, Our Loving Lord Jesus Christ, we ask you to bless, heal, and have mercy on Father _____. Blessing, honor, and glory to you, Redeemer King!

Our Father ...
Hail Mary ...
Glory Be ...

The Sixth Station: Veronica Wipes the Face of Jesus

V: We adore you, O Christ, and we bless you.
R: Because by your Holy Cross, you have redeemed the world.

Amen, I say to you, whatever you did for one of these least brothers of mine, you did for me. (Mattew 25:40)

The sweat and blood pouring down your face sting your eyes. We laud you amidst the jeers of onlookers. Veronica has compassion as she watches, and with a cloth, she gently touches your Holy Face. Your priest, too, needs kindness, understanding, and compassion when he is faced with difficulties.

In this moment, Our Loving Lord Jesus Christ, we ask you to bless, heal, and have mercy on Father _____. Blessing, honor, and glory to you, Redeemer King!

Our Father …
Hail Mary …
Glory Be …

The Seventh Station: Jesus Falls the Second Time

V: We adore you, O Christ, and we bless you.
R: Because by your Holy Cross, you have redeemed the world.

And many among them shall stumble;

fallen and broken;
snared and captured. (Isaiah 8:15)

The weight of the cross continues to push you down, Jesus, and this journey seems unending. It is hard to imagine that you have even more pain to endure! All the holy angels understand the agony suffered by the one and only God, but we look on in confusion. At this same moment, your priest has more pain to endure while living in this valley of tears. Help him arise with you, again and again, when his service feels too heavy a burden.

In this moment, Our Loving Lord Jesus Christ, we ask you to bless, heal, and have mercy on Father _____. Blessing, honor, and glory to you, Redeemer King!

Our Father …
Hail Mary …
Glory Be …

The Eighth Station: Jesus Consoles the Women

V: We adore you, O Christ, and we bless you.
R: Because by your Holy Cross, you have redeemed the world.

A large crowd of people followed Jesus, including many women who mourned and lamented him. Jesus turned to them and said, "Daughters of Jerusalem, do not weep for me; weep instead for yourselves and for your children, for indeed, the days are coming when people will say, 'Blessed are the barren, the wombs that never bore and the breasts that never nursed.' At that time people will say to the mountains, 'Fall upon us!' and to the hills, 'Cover us!' for if these things are done when the wood is green, what will happen when it is dry?" (Luke 23:27–31)

You look with kindness at the women who weep for you. You are battered and torn, yet you comfort us. Thank you, God! Give this priest grace to care for his flock even when he is faced with great challenges and suffering.

In this moment, Our Loving Lord Jesus Christ, we ask you to bless, heal, and have mercy on Father _____. Blessing, honor, and glory to you, Redeemer King!

Our Father …
Hail Mary …
Glory Be …

The Ninth Station:
Jesus Falls the Third Time

V: We adore you, O Christ, and we bless you.
R: Because by your Holy Cross, you have redeemed the world.

The valiant one whose steps are guided by the LORD,
  who will delight in his way,
May stumble, but he will never fall,
  for the LORD *holds his hand. (Psalm 37:23–24)*

Jesus, you have fallen again. We can hardly bear to see it! Although we can't understand all that is before us, we venerate you with our whole hearts. As you fall a third time, keep this priest from feeling despair when he feels battered by trials and tribulations.

In this moment, Our Loving Lord Jesus Christ, we ask you to bless, heal, and have mercy on Father _____. Blessing, honor, and glory to you, Redeemer King!

Our Father …
Hail Mary …
Glory Be …

The Tenth Station:
Jesus Is Stripped of His Garments

V: We adore you, O Christ, and we bless you.
R: Because by your Holy Cross, you have redeemed the world.

When the soldiers had crucified Jesus, they took his clothes and divided them into four shares, a share for each soldier. They also took his tunic, but the tunic was seamless, woven in one piece from the top down. So they said to one another, "Let's not tear it, but cast lots for it to see whose it will be," in order that the passage of scripture might be fulfilled [that says]: "They divided my garments among them, and for my vesture they cast lots." (John 19:23–24)

Jesus, they stripped you of your clothes in order to strip away your dignity. But since you are the one true king, you alone are exalted. Help your priest when he feels defenseless, or when his dignity has been tarnished.

In this moment, Our Loving Lord Jesus Christ, we ask you to bless, heal, and have mercy on Father _____. Blessing, honor, and glory to you, Redeemer King!

Our Father …
Hail Mary …

Glory Be …

The Eleventh Station:
Jesus Is Nailed to the Cross

V: We adore you, O Christ, and we bless you.
R: Because by your Holy Cross, you have redeemed the world.

When they came to the place called the Skull, they crucified him and the criminals there, one on his right, the other on his left. [Then Jesus said, "Father, forgive them, they know not what they do."] (Luke 23:33–34)

We watch with fear and trembling, Jesus, as nails are driven into your precious body. Witnessing the horror, we increase our praises to you. Forgive this priest, even in those times when he does something he deems unforgivable.

In this moment, Our loving Lord Jesus Christ, we ask you to bless, heal, and have mercy on Father _____. Blessing, honor, and glory to you, Redeemer King!

Our Father …
Hail Mary …
Glory Be …

The Twelfth Station: Jesus Dies on the Cross

V: We adore you, O Christ, and we bless you.

R: Because by your Holy Cross, you have redeemed the world.

It was now about noon and darkness came over the whole land until three in the afternoon because of an eclipse of the sun. Then the veil of the temple was torn down the middle. Jesus cried out in a loud voice, "Father, into your hands I commend my spirit"; and when he had said this he breathed his last. (Luke 23:44–46)

The world is dark, and time seems to stop. Although it seems there is no hope, we trust in you, Lord! Help this priest never to live in darkness without you, but always to remain in the light of the Holy Spirit.

In this moment, Our Loving Lord Jesus Christ, we ask you to bless, heal, and have mercy on Father _____. Blessing, honor, and glory to you, Redeemer King!

Our Father …
Hail Mary …
Glory Be …

The Thirteenth Station:
Jesus Is Taken Down from the Cross

V: We adore you, O Christ, and we bless you.
R: Because by your Holy Cross, you have redeemed the world.

They took the body of Jesus and bound it with burial cloths along with the spices, according to the Jewish burial custom. (John 19:40)

As your body is removed from the horrible cross, Jesus, we are reduced to silence. Sadness has overtaken us, but we remain your faithful children who find a way to praise you. Give this priest confidence that his sacrifices will bear fruit in eternity.

In this moment, Our Loving Lord Jesus Christ, we ask you to bless, heal, and have mercy on Father _____. Blessing, honor, and glory to you, Redeemer King!

> Our Father ...
> Hail Mary ...
> Glory Be ...

The Fourteenth Station:
Jesus Is Laid in the Sepulcher

V: We adore you, O Christ, and we bless you.

R: Because by your Holy Cross, you have redeemed the world.

Taking the body, Joseph wrapped it [in] clean linen and laid it in his new tomb that he had hewn in the rock. Then he rolled a huge stone across the entrance to the tomb and departed. (Matthew 27:59–60)

As your body is wrapped in the burial shroud, Jesus, our sadness is complete. Although we cannot comprehend what has occurred, and we believe that we have lost you, we trust in all you have taught us. In our sorrow, we still sing your praises. We beg you to give this priest his eternal reward in heaven on the last day.

In this moment, Our Loving Lord Jesus Christ, we ask you to bless, heal, and have mercy on Father _____. Blessing, honor, and glory to you, Redeemer King!

Our Father …
Hail Mary …
Glory Be …

Stations Closing Prayer

We thank you for this time meditating on your suffering and death, O Lord Jesus Christ. May our prayers give glory to you, Our Risen Lord. Blessing, honor, and glory to you, Redeemer King! Amen.

Help Him!

Holy Trinity, help Father _____ with his daily struggles.
God, in your kindness, deliver him.
Strengthen his virtues and help him to overcome his vices.
Enlarge his heart to be like yours.
Give him unfaltering faith.
Fill his mind with supernatural light.
Bless his physical senses.
Strengthen his memory.
Give him the graces he needs to attend to his own physical
    needs.
Comfort him when he is disturbed or grieving.
Invigorate him when he is fatigued, exhausted, or sad.
Give him zeal for your kingdom.
Give him the courage to fight for the truth.
Give him words of consolation.
Give him the grace to turn away from the deadly sins and
    increase within him the gifts and fruits of the Holy
    Spirit.

Give him the strength to carry his cross daily.

Have mercy on him!

He believes; help his unbelief.

Help him to contemplate heavenly things, despite living in this valley of tears.

Help him to believe in the power of prayer.

Help him to keep the Ten Commandments.

Help him to bear fruit with his vocation.

Help him to seek you with his whole heart, mind, and soul.

Help him to meditate on your law, day and night.

Help him to put forth his best efforts in his work.

Help him to be loyal, dedicated, and committed.

Help him to live united to the Blessed Trinity in his thoughts, words, and deeds.

Help him to teach, instruct, and encourage others.

Help him to overcome laziness.

Help him to be optimistic.

Help him to bear witness with his example.

Help him to fulfill his obligations cheerfully.

Help him to reflect your radiance.

Help him to appreciate the good things that have been given to him.

Help him to imitate the saints.

Help him to remember the top priorities of his vocation.

Help him through challenges, especially anger, sadness,

and frustration.

Help him to honor your Holy Name.

Help him in his different roles as pastor, consoler, teacher, and friend.

Help him to live the little moments of the day with you.

Help him to open the minds and hearts of others to the Scriptures.

Help him to not give in to discouragement.

Help him to remember why he became a priest.

Help him to keep his eyes on his eternal goal.

Help him to know when to speak and when to be silent.

Help him to be consistent with his faith.

Help him to have sincere devotion.

Help him to offer *all* to you.

Help him to be salt and light to the world by preserving your holy truths.

Help him to remember he is called to live joyously for love of you.

Help him gain his eternal crown and live with you for all eternity.

"May the God of peace himself make [Father _____] perfectly holy and may [he] entirely, spirit, soul, and body, be preserved blameless for the coming of our Lord Jesus Christ" (1 Thes 5:23).

Amen.

Closing Prayer

*To all the beloved of God in Rome, called to
be holy. Grace to you and peace from God
our Father and the Lord Jesus Christ.*

— Romans 1:7

Thank you, God, for this time in your holy presence.
Please accept my heartfelt prayers, and may they
bear fruit in the life of Father _____.

Our Father …
Hail Mary …
Glory Be …
All glory to God!
Amen.

Prayers of the Rosary

The Apostles' Creed
I believe in God,
the Father almighty,
Creator of heaven and earth,
and in Jesus Christ, his only Son, our Lord,
who was conceived by the Holy Spirit,
born of the Virgin Mary,
suffered under Pontius Pilate,
was crucified, died and was buried;
he descended into hell;
on the third day he rose again from the dead;
he ascended into heaven,
and is seated at the right hand of God the Father almighty;
from there he will come to judge the living and the dead.
I believe in the Holy Spirit,
the holy catholic Church,
the communion of saints,
the forgiveness of sins,

the resurrection of the body,
and life everlasting.
Amen.

Our Father

Our Father, who art in heaven, hallowed be thy name; thy kingdom come, thy will be done on earth as it is in heaven. Give us this day our daily bread, and forgive us our trespasses, as we forgive those who trespass against us; and lead us not into temptation, but deliver us from evil. Amen.

Hail Mary

Hail, Mary, full of grace, the Lord is with you. Blessed are you among women and blessed is the fruit of your womb, Jesus. Holy Mary, Mother of God, pray for us sinners, now and at the hour of our death. Amen.

Glory Be

Glory be to the Father and to the Son and to the Holy Spirit, as it was in the beginning, is now, and ever shall be, world without end. Amen.

Fatima Prayer

O my Jesus, forgive us our sins, save us from the fires of hell; lead all souls to heaven, especially those who have most need of your mercy.

Hail, Holy Queen

Hail, Holy Queen, mother of mercy, our life, our sweetness and our hope. To you we cry, poor banished children of Eve. To you we send up our sighs, mourning and weeping in this valley of tears. Turn then, most gracious advocate, your eyes of mercy toward us, and after this our exile, show unto us the blessed fruit of your womb, Jesus. O clement, O loving, O sweet Virgin Mary.

V. Pray for us, O holy Mother of God.
R. That we may be made worthy of the promises of Christ. Amen.

Closing Prayer

Let us pray: O God, whose only begotten Son, by his life, death, and resurrection, has purchased for us the rewards of eternal life, grant, we beseech thee, that while meditating on these mysteries of the most holy Rosary of the Blessed Virgin Mary, we may imitate what they contain and obtain what they promise, through the same Christ Our Lord. Amen.

Acknowledgments

In thanksgiving for my husband, Dan, who supports me in any endeavor I undertake. I am blessed beyond measure for our shared faith, cross, and friendship. For our sons, Danny, Harrison, and Anthony, who have inspired this work in countless ways.

I am grateful for the wise priests who have impacted my family, especially those who have been good friends and true fathers to us. To Msgr. Lawrence B. McInerny, thank you for inspiring this book and being such a faithful shepherd.

I am profoundly grateful to Jamie Pohlman, to my critique group (especially Vijaya Bodach, Janeen Zaio, Michelle Shahid, and Deana Lattanzio), and to my "Seven Sisters," especially Eileen Kittrell and Mimi Gaeta.

I am thankful for Mary Beth Giltner, Elizabeth Scalia, and to everyone at OSV.

Finally, I thank all the faithful and loving friends and family who have prayed for me. I give thanks to God for you!

About the Author

Tina Jost lives in Charleston, South Carolina, and is a devoted wife and mother to three grown sons. She received her BA in psychology in 1995 and then went on to homeschool her children. Tina is a Catholic writer for *Radiant* magazine and *The Catholic Miscellany*, a life coach, a professional workshop facilitator, and a Catholic Writer's Guild member. As an anchoress for the Seven Sisters Apostolate, she is committed to praying fervently for one priest each week during adoration of the Blessed Sacrament.

You might also like:

How to Pray:
A Practical Guide to the Spiritual Life
By David Torkington

If we want to become the people God made us to be, we need to set aside time every day for prayer. It sounds simple enough, but we often allow distractions, temptations, and our busy lives to keep us from daily prayer.

In this book, spiritual theologian David Torkington offers everyday guidance for entering more deeply into prayer, whether you are a beginner or looking to go deeper in your prayer life. The forty short, easy-to-read chapters in this guide can be read as a devotional, for meditation, or alongside Sacred Scripture.